Y

W9-AWC-386

3 3028 00594 4436

MISHAWAKA

WITHDRAWN
From the
Mishawaka - Penn - Harris Public Library

Mishawaka-Penn-Harris Public Library
Mishawaka, Indiana

GAYLORD M

J. Patrick Lewis

SCIEN-TRICKERY

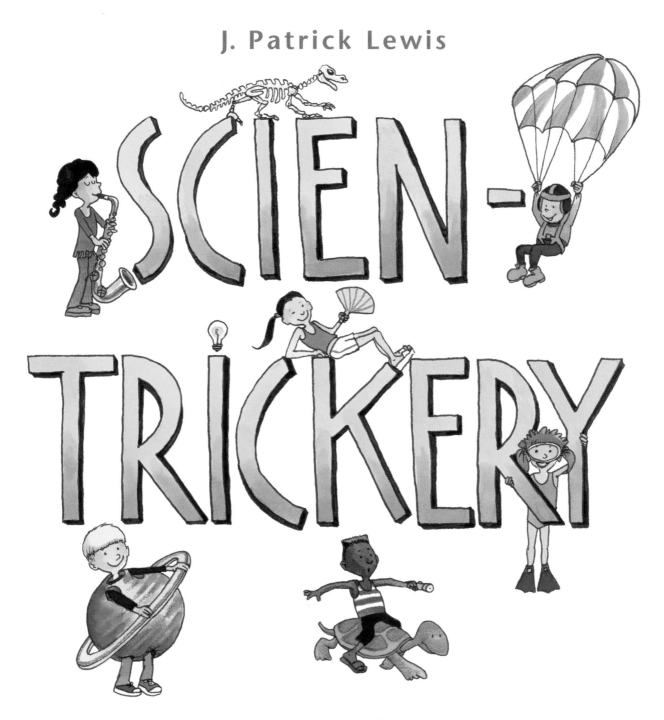

Riddles in Science

Illustrated by Frank Remkiewicz

Silver Whistle
Harcourt, Inc.

Orlando   Austin   New York   San Diego

**Mishawaka-Penn-Harris
Public Library
Mishawaka, Indiana**

For Claudia and Mary—J. P. L.

For Andreas Birkedal-Hansen.
Thanks for your formulae for success—F. R.

Text copyright © 2004 by J. Patrick Lewis
Illustrations copyright © 2004 by Frank Remkiewicz

All rights reserved. No part of this publication may be reproduced or transmitted in any form or by any means, electronic or mechanical, including photocopy, recording, or any information storage and retrieval system, without permission in writing from the publisher.

Requests for permission to make copies of any part of the work should be mailed to the following address: Permissions Department, Harcourt, Inc., 6277 Sea Harbor Drive, Orlando, Florida 32887-6777.

www.HarcourtBooks.com

Silver Whistle is a trademark of Harcourt, Inc., registered in the United States of America and/or other jurisdictions.

Library of Congress Cataloging-in-Publication Data
Lewis, J. Patrick.
Scien-trickery: riddles in science/J. Patrick Lewis; illustrated by Frank Remkiewicz.
p. cm.
Summary: A collection of poems that describes people, places, and things associated with science, including oxygen, the ocean, and germs.
1. Science—Juvenile poetry. 2. Children's poetry, American. [1. Science—Poetry. 2. American poetry.]
I. Remkiewicz, Frank, ill. II. Title.
PS3562.E9465S38 2004
811'.54—dc21 2002153962
ISBN 0-15-216681-5

First edition
H G F E D C B A
Manufactured in China

The illustrations in this book were rendered in watercolor and Prisma colored pencils on Bristol Board.
The display type was created by Frank Remkiewicz.
The text type was set in Lemonade Bold.
Color separations by Bright Arts Ltd., Hong Kong
Manufactured by South China Printing Company, Ltd., China
This book was printed on totally chlorine-free Stora Enso Matte paper.
Production supervision by Sandra Grebenar and Ginger Boyer
Designed by Frank Remkiewicz, Judythe Sieck, and Suzanne Fridley

CONTENTS

FLIGHTLESS
CORMORANT

FUR SEALS

BEAGLE

SHORT-EARED OWL

MOCKING-THRUSH

GOLDEN WARBLER

VERMILION FLYCATCHER

Shell Game

Here is where
The giant tortoise
Moves as slow as
Rigor mortis.

Darwin studied
Awesome fauna—
Finches, cormo-
rants, iguanas

On this scien-
tific shore
Off the coast of
Ecuador.

ANSWER: Galápagos Islands

GIANT TORTOISES

MARINE IGUANA

5

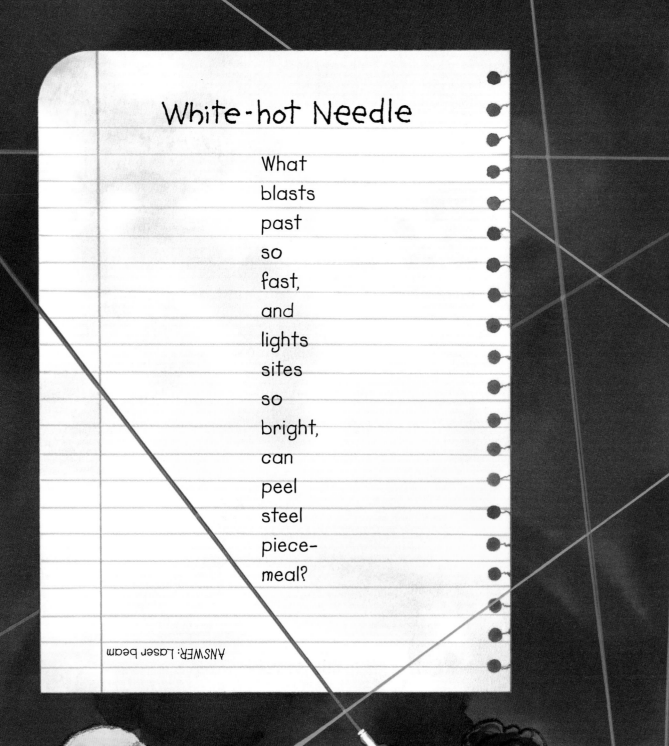

White-hot Needle

What
blasts
past
so
fast,
and
lights
sites
so
bright,
can
peel
steel
piece-
meal?

ANSWER: Laser beam

Buggety Buggety Boo!

Though each of us is smaller than a flea,
We've spread all over since eternity
(But you might think we come
    from Germany).

You know the sniffles, sneezes, and the flu
Because we've introduced them all to you.
We are the microscopic you-know-who!

ANSWER: Germs

AE = VIP

An absolutely famous guy,
He showed us all the reason why,
By flying super fast, you know,
Your watch runs relatively slow.

Giant among the brilliant giants,
He wrote formulas for science.
So amazing, they contain
Stuff exclusively for brains!

ANSWER: Albert Einstein

Push Me, Pull Me

"Say, what if we two," she insisted,
"Could stick together?" He resisted.

Their north poles jitterbugged and may
Have touched . . . but quickly pushed away.

And so they tried to make a start
From south to south . . . still far apart.

Turning around and facing north,
She threw her little metal forth!

Kaaa-thwupp! Those two engaging chips
Were stuck like barnacles to ships.

ANSWER: Magnets

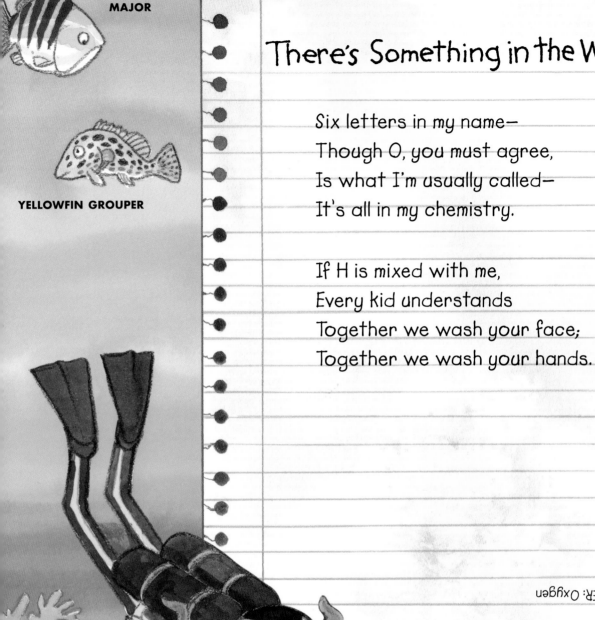

SERGEANT MAJOR

YELLOWFIN GROUPER

There's Something in the Water

Six letters in my name—
Though O, you must agree,
Is what I'm usually called—
It's all in my chemistry.

If H is mixed with me,
Every kid understands
Together we wash your face;
Together we wash your hands.

ANSWER: Oxygen

RED GROUPER

Gee !

It keeps you from flying
　　Off into space.
It's what makes you fall
　　Flat on your face.
And if it could talk
　　Like you and I do,
I think it would say,
　　"I'm pulling for you."

ANSWER: Gravity

13

The Old Switcheroo

My father's the arc,
My mother's the spark.
Without *them* you would
Be left in the dark.

ANSWER: Electricity

14

You'll N·E·ver Guess What's N·E·xt

I begin with N-E,
And I'm one of nine.
I end with N-E,
And I'm eighth in line.

ANSWER: Neptune

I'm Lost without You

Should I head south? Or travel north?
I'm undecided. Back or forth?

I put my trust in compass Sun,
Which has returned me to square one.

I *know* this road three cows have crossed.
The cows are ambling home. ....*I'm lost.*

But I could get home easily
If I'd brought one of these with me.

ANSWER: A map

A Threat of Sweat

Whenever
    you visit
        Miami,
What is it
    that makes you
        so clammy?

ANSWER: Humidity

Nothing Doing

For those who like arithmetricks,
This fits inside 306

And looks like something that
  you know
Must end a word like *buffalo.*

It's not an egg that's standing tall.
(It isn't anything at all.)

ANSWER: Zero

YOUR WEIGHT 5¢

Revealing Ceiling

When we go into hiding,
Most nights are unexciting,
But that will change providing
    You let us entertain.

Delighting you, igniting
Way up here by highlighting!
We thank you for inviting
    Us through your windowpane.

ANSWER: Stars, starlight, or constellations

22

POLARIS

URSA MINOR

URSA MAJOR

Shhhhhhhhhh!

I am expressible
Only by decibel:

10 is a whisper,
30 is crisper,
60, in relation,
Is normal conversation.
80 is traffic and telephones.
120? The Rolling Stones.
130 is a cannon shot!

150 is... *what?!*

ANSWER: Sound

Salt Cellar

A quilt of blue on blue,
   Ten thousand ships' good-byes,
      A shattered mirror to
         The self-important skies?
            The city of the strange,
               The country of the deep?
                  The wind's first practice range,
               The secret seagulls keep?
            The home to buried hills?
         Oh, what's a mystery for?
      This empire that builds
   Gold borders on a shore.

ANSWER: Ocean

26

SPANISH HOGFISH

IGUANODON

28

T-bones

Sixty-five million years ago,
All of them were left behind.
But they still stomp and they still roar
Around the corners of your mind.

ANSWER: Dinosaurs

It's the Pits!

Oh, I eat iron, chrome, and steel,
And I chew tin with every meal.

My mouth grows larger as I'm fed.
My lips are turning orangy red.

Car fenders? *Yum!* Front bumpers, cheers!
My dinners last for years and years.

ANSWER: Rust

30

Go, Moon, Glow!

"I'll hide my face!" says Moon, says she,
    "Sun will think I'm gone."
"Now, where is Moon," says Sun, says he,
    "to shine my light upon?"

Several minutes then go by....
    How soon will Moon appear?
Says Moon, "How I enjoy this dark
    Celestial atmosphere!"

It's all because the earth has flown
    Between the moon and sun.
But wait a second! There's a slice
    Of Moon for everyone.

ANSWER: Lunar eclipse

31

NOTES

Shell Game

Six hundred miles west of Ecuador lie the Galápagos Islands, made famous in 1835 by Charles Darwin (1809-1882) after his voyage there on HMS Beagle. Darwin studied all kinds of animals and plants there to support his theory of evolution.

White-hot Needle

Laser is an acronym for light amplification by stimulated emission of radiation. One of the greatest inventions of the twentieth century, the laser is a device that emits an intense beam of light that can penetrate extremely hard substances—like steel. You can only begin to imagine all the uses of a laser beam in industry, medicine, telecommunications, scientific research, and military operations!

AE = VIP

Very Important Person, indeed! Albert Einstein (1879-1955) is probably best known for his theories of relativity. One of the most creative thinkers of the twentieth century, Einstein is generally credited with changing the way we think about the universe. Time magazine named him "Person of the Century."

Push Me, Pull Me

North and south are commonly used to refer to poles of a magnet. Similar poles resist each other, but opposites attract.

There's Something in the Water

Scientists abbreviate the gas hydrogen as H_2 and the gas oxygen as O_2. Mixing hydrogen and oxygen together creates water, which is abbreviated as H_2O.

Gee!

Gravity is simply the force that draws bodies toward the earth.

The Old Switcheroo

What causes the lights to go on when you pull the switch? Electricity! It arises because very tiny particles possess something called charge, and they move very quickly to create an arc or a spark, which is electricity.

You'll N-E-ver Guess What's N-E-xt

The eighth of nine planets from the sun, and the fourth largest planet (in diameter), Neptune has been visited by only one spacecraft (so far): Voyager 2, on August 24, 1989. Neptune's winds are the fastest in the solar system at 1,500 miles per hour.

A Threat of Sweat

In the rainforest, everything is saturated with a kind of wet heat. Turn toward the desert and you find a world of dry heat. Why? Differing humidity, or moisture content in the atmosphere.

Nothing Doing

The invention of zero was the greatest achievement in the development of a number system. Without it, astronomy, chemistry, and physics would be at a complete loss. We have the Hindu mathematicians who lived in India during the fifth and sixth centuries to thank for it.

Revealing Ceiling

Stars are actually hot spheres of gas, and they shine because of the energy produced by chemical reactions. In the night sky, you can see several dozens of stars, but the universe contains trillions of them.

Shhhhhhhhhh!

Sound is created when an object moves, even just a little. The movement causes a disturbance, which radiates outward through the air in waves. When the waves reach your ear, what you hear is a sound.

Salt Cellar

Now here's a fact: Water covers 71 percent of Earth's surface. We have given the oceans names: Atlantic, Indian, Pacific, and Arctic. The oceans are where life on Earth first occurred three billion years ago.

T-bones

Dinosaur is a Greek word meaning "terrible lizard." From the many discoveries of their bones, we know just how large the dinosaurs were.

It's the Pits

Rust is the chemical deterioration of a metal, usually caused by contact with water or oxygen.

Go, Moon, Glow!

When the earth blocks the sun's light to the moon, there is a lunar eclipse. When the moon blocks the sun's light to the earth, there is a solar eclipse. Lunar eclipses are more common but can only occur when the moon is full.